# Self Help to Self Harm; The Dubious Guide to Life, Love, and Relationships

TOSHA MICHELLE

ISBN: 0692417400
ISBN-13: 978-0692417409 (La Literati)

# FOREWORD

Tosha Michelle is a dear friend, whom I respect deeply. I count her among my dearest allies and cherish the woman she is.

The words she uses when she writes gives the reader a glimpse into her soul and who she is at her deepest level. She has a delightful sense of humor but mixes it with a high level of intelligence and sophistication that causes her words to leap off the page, stabbing the heart of the reader and forcing us to feel what she feels or think what she thinks.

Tosha is the kind of person who will cry with you, rejoice with you and walk with you no matter what obstacles hinder your path. She is a treasure to the human race, someone you can trust with complete abandon and a determined and gifted writer. It is more than a pleasure to call her my friend.

-- Todd Lowe, Author of This Road I Travel

# CONTENTS

# INTRODUCTION

"A serious and good philosophical work could be written consisting entirely of jokes." -Ludwig Wittgenstein

Dear Reader,

This is not a self-help book. Sadly, this book won't get you laid, help you lose weight or cure your One Direction addiction. Okay, maybe, that's my addiction. Shh. I'm not an expert at anything unless you count tripping up the stairs, getting lost in my own head and devouring a box of Godiva chocolates in one sitting.

Now that I have told you what this book is not, let me tell you what I hope the book is. It supposed to be a humorous, tongue-in-cheek look at life, love, and relationships, tempered by moments of serious introspection.

It's kind of random and chaotic like its author. Oh, and you should know, I kind of have a list fetish. Don't say I didn't warn ya.

Tosha

TOSHA MICHELLE

# CHAPTER 1

## HELLO HANDSOME

An Open Letter to Men

We don't want to see the little engine that could. The clothes hamper exists for a reason. USE IT! We don't care how your mom did it. Asking for directions is not a sign of weakness. We don't always want to be on top. Use tools. Don't be a tool. The greatest gift you can give us is your time. If not your time, your wallet will suffice (I just lost my feminist card). You don't have to be our hero... just be there. Use your eyes less and your ears more. Listen to us...

and know....

We love you for your boyish enthusiasm. The way your hand fits in the small of our backs…your protective nature. How easily you let go of things and don't dwell on the past…your morning voice and sleepy eyes…the way you smell fresh out of the shower…your strength…your mind and your wit…your hard lines and edges…We adore you in suits…or a ratty college sweatshirt…or just in your boxers …the way you're the big spoon to our little spoon, and for just being all manly and hot…

but…pick your freaking clothes UP!

PS Tips and Dips

1. Love us for our hearts and minds, and we'll rock you with our bodies.
2. It is OK to be sensitive. Tears are not a sign of weakness…unless you're crying because you have nothing to wear, or you missed a Real Housewives episode.
3. There are two places tighty whities belong: on babies, or in the trash.
4. The vacuum cleaner and mop will not bite you. Go ahead. Try them on for size. I dare you.
5. Sometimes all we need to hear is "No, honey, let me do it."
6. Cologne is sexy, but no need to bathe in it.

7. A kiss on the hand at the right time can be quite lovely, at the wrong time, equally as creepy.

8. By all means, be the man in the relationship when it comes to killing bugs, or opening jars. We don't mind.

9. However, never tell us what to do. EVER!

10. We want to be your muses but not in a sleazy photographer kind of way. We long to bring out your inner Shakespeare, not Larry Flynt.

11. Withhold nothing. We need to know where all the carbon goes, and why prime numbers remain a mystery. I'm looking at you, Riemann hypothesis. Why is it all so weird? Oh, and everyone you have ever dated, and what you had for lunch, and how your day was, and what your brother said on the phone, etc.

12. Your mother was right, manners matter. Prove to us chivalry is not dead.

13. Please don't tell us to calm down. You calm down!

14. I mentioned this previously but felt the need to reiterate, no, we do not want to see a picture of the little engine that could.

15. Just because your friends might find us appealing doesn't mean we want to be with them. Well, unless your friends are Timothy Olyphant or Jon Stewart.

16. Please talk about your feelings. We want to know what's going on in those heads of yours. However, we don't have to have a come to Jesus meeting or an Oprah moment.
17. Douchebaggery is never a winning look. Wear compassion and humanity instead.
18. There's nothing hotter than a man with tools, unless it's a man with a book.
19. We like wearing your old college sweatshirt or sleeping in your T-shirt. Prepare to share. It makes us feel close to you.
20. All we need is affection, attention, love, chocolate -- and a guy with a big.........

brain.

## Ten Things Women Wish Men Knew

1.  We women like to be taken, but not in a way that requires our fathers to bring out their particular set of skills. You know, the ones they have acquired over their long career. No, we want be taken up against the wall, on the kitchen counter, on your desk, etc. We love to feel wanted and desirable.
2.  Pet names can be very sweet. However, don't make them too cutesy. There's nothing sexy about being called Kissy Kibbles, Schnookums or Licky Sticky Poo.
3.  It is never appropriate to call us a b*tch or by your ex-girlfriend's name.
4.  You don't fake foreplay. We won't fake an orgasm.
5.  Ladies first. See number 4.
6.  There's something extremely sexy about a man who can recite Shakespeare while listening to Bach as he fixes a leaky pipe.
7.  Be romantic. Note, sometimes being romantic simply means doing the laundry.
8.  Listen to us, dam*it
9.  You're adorable when you are shaving, driving, being kind to your mother, holding a baby, etc.
10. Love us. Respect us. Protect us. Do us.

## Ten Compliments We Never Tire of Hearing

1. I love your Jimmy Choo shoes.
   (Payless actually, but thanks.)
2. You've lost weight.
   (My winter clothes work wonders.)
3. You're a culinary master.
   (I call my technique take-out.)
4. You're a natural beauty.
   (Thanks. It took me an hour to perfect this look.)
5. Are you a dancer?
   (My best move is tripping up the stairs.)
6. I could listen to you talk for hours.
   (Good, because I have a litany of items to discuss.)
7. You're so witty.
   (Ugh, the pressure!)
8. You look so Italian?
   (Grazie mille!)
9. Your mind is a thing of beauty.
   (It is, isn't it?)
10. You were right.
    (Told you so)

# CHAPTER 2

## WHAT'S UP, GIRL?

An Open Letter to Women

"Women and cats will do as they please, and men and dogs should relax and get used to the idea."
— Robert A. Heinlein

Go forth and be fabulous.

Ok, I can't let us off that easily. I begrudging offer you things men wished women knew (blah, blah, blah)

1. Don't assume your guy knows what you are thinking. Talk to him. Just make sure to hide the remote first.
2. Don't mother him unless he has some kind of freaky Oedipus complex going on.

3. If you like a guy, let him know. Don't play mind game unless it is Trivial Pursuit.

4. Most men like the natural look as long as you don't look like Nature Boy Rick Flair

5. He's rarely going to turn down sex. No. Really.

6. Sometimes they just say what they think we want to hear.

7. He likes when you look hot.

8. Just not in front of his parents.

9. Ponytails

10. The quickest way to his heart is not through his stomach. It's through football.

11. He doesn't know what she said or he thinks or they did.

12. He needs his guy time.

13. Cook for him on occasion but make him clean up.

14. Sometimes let him pick the movie.

15. He doesn't need to know you are bloated.

16. Men can get emotional too. Just because he's not bawling after watching The Notebook doesn't mean he doesn't feel.

17. Sometimes he acts like a jerk because he is insecure and sometimes he is just a jerk.

# CHAPTER 3

## WE GO TOGETHER

Dear Men and Women,

Sex shouldn't be a commodity or used as leverage or bait. It shouldn't be a means of exploitation or slut shaming. It should be consensual and physical but not one dimensional.

For me, it's spiritual, soulful, an expression of life and love. It is emotion rooted in commitment and true intimacy. Society encourages us to settle for less. The media, music, television, tells us sex is just a feel good feeling. Pleasure alone. But true fulfillment comes when we combine the physical with the emotional.

This is just one flawed romantic's view.

Soul Mates -- The Pot, The Kettle, The Pea, the Pod and a Cat.

Ah, soul mates. The stuff chick flicks and Hallmark cards are made of. But who are these elusive creatures really? I don't necessarily equate a soul mate with hearts and flowers or sexual chemistry. In my opinion, soul mates come in many forms friends, parents, siblings, lovers, chocolate, my cat. ;)

Soul mates come into our lives to teach us something: how to laugh, think, feel, be, love, and often, how to let go. They enable us to grow emotionally, spiritually, and mentally.

These relationships are intense, magnetic, inexplicable, mystical and based on a strong connection. I can count my soul mates on one hand. But I'm an introvert, and although I love humanity, I'm not often that crazy about people. It takes a lot for me to genuinely bond, but when I do it sticks. I'm grateful for my soul mates and the lessons learned. They've enriched my soul and left indelible impressions on my heart.

Elizabeth Gilbert, in Eat, Pray, Love, describes the soul mate relationship best…

"People think a soul mate is your perfect fit, and that's what everyone wants. But a true soul mate is a mirror, the person who shows you everything that is holding you back, the person who brings you to your own attention so you can change your life.

A true soul mate is probably the most important person you'll ever meet, because they tear down your walls and smack you awake. But to live with a soul mate forever? Nah. Too painful. Soul mates, they come into your life just to reveal another layer of yourself to you, and then leave.

A soul mate's purpose is to shake you up, tear apart your ego a little bit, show you your obstacles and addictions, break your heart open so new light can get in, make you so desperate and out of control that you have to transform your life, then introduce you to your spiritual master…"

"Unending Love"

I seem to have loved you in numberless forms, numberless times…
In life after life, in age after age, forever.
My spellbound heart has made and remade the necklace of songs,

That you take as a gift, wear round your neck in
your many forms,

In life after life, in age after age, forever.

Whenever I hear old chronicles of love, it's age
old pain,

It's ancient tale of being apart or together.

As I stare on and on into the past, in the end you
emerge,

Clad in the light of a pole-star, piercing the
darkness of time.

You become an image of what is remembered
forever.

You and I have floated here on the stream that
brings from the fount

At the heart of time, love of one for another.

We have played alongside millions of lovers,

Shared in the same shy sweetness of meeting,

the distressful tears of farewell,

Old love, but in shapes that renew and renew
forever.

Today it is heaped at your feet, it has found its
end in you

The love of all man's days both past and forever:

Universal joy, universal sorrow, universal life.

Rules to Get Through Another Hallmark Holiday aka Valentine's Day.

1.  Flowers picked, not bought. Any idiot can call the florist. It takes a special idiot to go out and create his own bouquet of suck up.
2.  Absolutely no gifts from CVS or Walgreens
3.  No plush toys unless they are of the adult variety.
4.  The same applies for appliances.
5.  A card is a must. Extra points for a homemade one with a love letter inside.
6.  Ladies, break out the sexy underwear or better yet, no underwear.
7.  Also, girls, no personal ads to your snuggly, buggly, baby boo…. especially if it's the first date.
8.  Gentlemen, no gifts inside a ring size box, unless it's actually a ring…a really, big ring…
9.  If you are alone and single on Valentine's Day or married and alone, (hey, you never know) kick Cupid to the curb, grab a friend and go out and celebrate YOU.
10. Make love the star of the show all the time, not just on some commercial cliché holiday made popular by Hallmark. Love is alive and all around us. Take time to experience and

bask in its presence every day of your existence. Embrace love. Feel love. Be love.

# CHAPTER 4

## YES. NO. MAYBE.

This list is for when you have gotten roped into a date and need to get out of it. Remember, people tongue in cheek

Creative Excuses to Get Out of a Date

1. My sister-in-law's friend's cousin's father's uncle tragically lost his pet turtle. The details are just too sordid to share.
2. My re-gifting recipient list demands to be written. Christmas will be here again before you know it.
3. I've fallen. I could get up, but I refuse.
4. I never go on a date on days that end with day.
5. My cat won't let me.
6. I have to attend Charles Manson's wedding.

7. I've been meaning to get a Rob Ford tattoo on my shoulder and it can't wait.
8. I'm just way too busy chewing gum.
9. I have an important call from a telemarketer, and I HAVE to take it.
10. I've been putting off making my Justin Bieber scrapbook. (Bieber fever won't wait)
11. It just wouldn't be fair to all the other beautiful people.
12. Summer will be here before you know it. I need to work out. Those Speedos won't wear themselves.
13. I've been putting off reading Fifty Shades of Grey. E.L. James is calling to me.
14. Signing up for an AOL account. It is way overdue.
15. I've being dying to take a beets bath.
16. My diet has been sorely lacking in kale lately. I must eat some NOW.
17. I need to spend some serious time thinking up more excuses for why I can't go on this date.
18. I'm writing a new book on sardines and I have a deadline to meet.
19. Ke$ha is in town for one day only. I can't miss this concert.
20. I need to get a restraining order. How do you spell your name again?

However, suppose you have met the guy or girl of your dreams, and getting out of the date is the last thing you want. Where should you take your new love? What should you do?

Creative Date Ideas. OK, "somewhat" creative.

1. A hot air balloon ride. (cheesy, I know) Just make sure you trust the person. It is a long way down.
2. A Ghost Walk
3. Dinner with your mom. (kidding) How about zip lining it down a mountain?
4. A stroll through a historic town.
5. Attend an art class together.
6. Hop on a train and see the countryside.
7. A sex club (kidding, again, unless that is your thing, if it is, you dirty little git.) Note, I like to pretend I am English on occasion and use British slang. I know, bloody hell.)
8. Take your date down by the river. Leave the van.
9. Picnic anywhere.
10. Attend an open house.
11. Write a song together and perform it
12. Go to the airport and watch planes take off.
13. Fly a kite.

14. Get drunk at a winery.
15. Go to a bookstore and pick out a book to read together.
16. Volunteer at a soup kitchen.
17. Go on hike.
18. Cook a meal together.
19. Have your fortune told.
20. Star glazing at observatory.
21. Express your inner furry, and go to the Humane Society. (If your inner furry, like to dress up as a lamb, I don't want to know.)
22. Swing dancing.
23. Dive bar
24. Famers Market
25. An art gallery.
26. A petting zoo
27. Crash a wedding (or a funeral) ;)
28. Stalk a celebrity. (Timothy Olyphant, I'm looking at you!)
29. Attend a concert in the park.
30. Create your own philosophy or language.
31. Enroll in Clown College.
32. Reenact Fifty Shades of Grey.
33. Attend a poetry slam.
34. People watch at an outdoor café. Make up backstories for them.
35. Have a water fight.

# CHAPTER 5

## OH YOU NASTY BOYS

### Bad Boys, Bad Boys. What You Gonna Do?

Why are women (some women) attracted to bad boys? What makes a sensible, intelligent woman lose her head over a man who only knows one mode-jerk? I think there are a few reasons. The thrill of the chase, the need to nurture and "fix" the man. "If I just love him enough, he will change" There's also an element of danger and excitement that comes from being with rebel without nice bone in his body.

How do these relationships usually end, badly. We can't change a man who docsn't want to. There are only so many times we can bail him out of jail, or catch him a lie and not lose our sh**. The endless conflict and turmoil is not worth the hassle.

How can a nice guy compete with a bad boy? It's simple, have the bad boy swagger without the bad boy ways. Remember, confidence is sexy. Self-respect is a must. Don't worry about always saying the right thing, just be real and genuine. Take charge but don't be controlling. At the end of the day, nice guys don't have to finish last; they just have to start strong.

# CHAPTER 6

## DID YOU FALL FROM HEAVEN?

Who among us hasn't been on the receiving end of a cheesy pick-up line? What self-help parody book would be complete without including some God awful ones? The following were submitted by readers worldwide. Some are really original. Enjoy.

I'm desperate; you're here... wanna try to make me happy? –Michael G.

On Match.com a man messaged me & commented on my little extra weight: "Looks like the little extra is in all the right places" –SF

"Hey good looking. What those mile long legs got cooking!" ~ College frat boys. I was fourteen camping with my parents at a campground in southern Virginia; hence you must imagine the accent. - Amy H. Peterson

"Hey you look like my Mom when she was young and my dad said she was hot and sexy"-- Janice

Heard from a male colleague back when I was a financial futures trader in London. "My face is leaving in 5 minutes. Be on it." –Mark

If you were a triangle, you would be acute one- Jennifer Chase

I thought I'd be clever... I once told a date: "You're no good on either side of a camera".- Gabby

My father asked my mother: "How would you like to be buried with my folks?"-Larry

I once told a hot man in a Philly Chinese restaurant "I can handle your moo shu "guy" pan no matter how hot it gets". Attribute me so I can awesome it up! –Sandra

I feel like we've met before. Always hoped I would see you again- Donna Tibbett Stevens

Honey, you have the kind of legs I love. Feet on one end, and hoochie on the other.- R. Laurence White, Southern Gentleman's Club

In college, I was manager of the student union building. While working one night, a girl approached & told me I had beautiful hair. "I'm an artist & would love to paint your portrait." And before I could answer, she added, "By the way, are you seeing anyone?"-Vinny

"You have more of a rubenesque figure."-Stephanie

One time this guy said to me...your dad must have been a thief... I said huh? He said looks like he stole all the stars from the sky and put them in your eyes.-S.

I can't believe none of them worked.- Arioch

"I once had a headache and seeing a pretty girl just took it away." "Really? When?" "Just now, *wink*"-Gina C.

When I was 21, a very attractive, older woman... (7 years older, maybe)... told me, "I'd hate to see you have a fight with your wife and then drive around angry all night... when you could be spending the night with me!" (She went on to become a very successful... famous... artist and sculptress, whose name I would certainly never share, out of respect. But a very talented and "creative" woman, I've always thought. Sweet memories.)-Skip

"Do you kiss your mother with that mouth?" Followed by a suggestive -- and creepy -- wink.-Gabe Howard

Girl approached me and said, "Hi. My name is Bend Over." True story-Todd

I've been waiting for you ALL my life." My response, "Guess you have another long wait." -Catherine

"I thought you were gay"- David Warriet Edwards

"Me Tarzan. You Jane.-Jane

"Lay down Baby I believe I love you!" – Annette

Back in my college days I remember this one corny line someone said to me at a club. "Girl, you're like the sun, you make me hot"-Sheri

A few years ago when I was out with friends at a bar, a guy about 20 years younger than me noticed my wedding band on my finger....looked at me and asked if I'd like to be his Mrs. Robinson....I thought that was quite clever.-Sandy

Could you kill my boyfriend for me?-Derek

# CHAPTER 7

## KEYS TO A HAPPY RELATIONSHIP

1. Lots of alcohol.
2. Denial
3. Lies. Lies. Lies.

I suppose if I have to seriously answer how to make a relationship work. I would first reiterate: I am not an expert on relationships. Drink every time you read relationship. However, it seems to be the tenants of a healthy partnership are rooted in respect, open communication, and the art of compromise. Here's a few of my thoughts on what it takes to make love last. Take them with a grain of salt and spoonful of Nutella.

1. You don't always have to be right. It's not about winning an argument. It's about putting the relationship before pride and anger.

2. "I love you" should be said often and with meaning.
3. Make time for each other. Look at one another, talk, hold hands, and connect. The football game can be recorded, the laundry can wait.
4. Never lose sight of love, even when you want to punch your mate in the nose.
5. Never punch your mate in the nose. ☺
6. Always be honest. Temper the honesty with kindness.
7. Know how to have fun together.
8. Never stop courting your mate.
9. Secrets are a no-no.
10. Take new adventures together.
11. Make time for intimacy.
12. Ask questions. Take an interest in your partner's life and feelings.
13. Remember neither of you are perfect.
14. Be positive.
15. It takes two to make a happy couple or a miserable divorce.

What is Real Love?

Once upon a time in a land called Life. There lived a thing called Real Love. Now, it is true that Real Love is often the stuff fairy tales are made of. It can only last so long running off fairy dust.

Real Love, the lasting kind, is always firmly rooted in reality. You see, even the Prince and Princess would argue over crowns being left on the floor and how to run the kingdom. They understood that to live happily ever after, they had to accept that Real Love is not just butterflies, hearts and flowers. Sometimes it feels more like bee stings, rain and quicksand.

Real Love is made up of things like commitment, compromise, consistency, loyalty, riding the highs and the lows, and hard work. It's about trust and allowing each other to grow and BE. Real Love creates its own kind of magic and tenacity. It is sacred, profane, mundane, extraordinary, heaven and hell, and the only love worth fighting for. Sadly, Real Love is hard to find and even harder to hold on to.

TOSHA MICHELLE

# CHAPTER 8

## THE TANGLED WEB-MY JOURNEY TO THE CENTER OF THE INTERNET

The year was 1999 and I was still very much a baby, at least emotionally. You see, I had always led a cloistered and sheltered life, a relativity happy life; blessed in many ways. It's as if I had stepped right out of an Austen novel, however, this was a difficult year for me, the hardest of my life in fact. This was the year I walked straight into a Bronte narrative, Emily's not Charlotte's. I was struggling both emotionally and physically. My situation made me a hot mess of crazy (as opposed to my usual quirky mess of nutty). My emotions were all over the place and the quarter life crisis was in full swing. Good times, y'all.

Have I set this up enough? Do you get the picture? Imagine "All About Eve" meets "Brian's Song". It was the year of my discontent that I discovered the web and all its mysteries. I was like a kid in a candy store, a very innocent and fragile kid. The internet opened up a whole new world for me and I met some really interesting characters. One would become a lifelong friend and to this day is like a sister to me. The other came into my life for a season to guide and teach me some valuable lessons about myself and the world at large. Lessons that took a while to take hold. I'm nothing if not stubborn. This person taught me to be real with myself, to be honest. They helped me find parts that were lost, they showed me parts I had hidden away, they exposed things I did not wish to look at yet needed to and they encouraged me to believe in myself. Through their support, I learned to stand on my own two feet and found my voice. I learned I had more courage than I thought and discovered an inner strength I never knew I possessed. I learned to appreciate what I have and to live life to the fullest with no regrets, no excuses and no looking back. They also taught me how to let go of fear, guilt, anger, and the hot mess crazy side of myself. On a trivial note, it was from them that I acquired my love for "The Princess Bride"

Both these people were my anchors and life lines. They helped me reconnect with my authentic self and discover new levels and depths to my personality. Of course they had to put up with a lot of drama and angst too. I will forever be grateful for their support. I will always remember their kindness and how they were a catalyst for major changes in my life, all for the better.

It was also through the internet that I met my friends, Jane, Niles, and Mr. Lovely himself Colin. These relationships have morphed into real life. What a blessing. I am forever indebted to Jane for always being a sounding board, my soul sister and partner in crime. She makes me laugh and amazes me with her tenacity and spunk. She's beautiful inside and out and the ying to my yang. Niles is my brother from another mother and my eternal introverted bibliophile buddy. He's a quiet, gentle soul full of knowledge and kindness. Then there Colin he is my mentor and a myriad of the mystic and profound. It is through him that I have learned so much about humanity. He inspired me to become an advocate, to do more, expect more and be more.

I suppose with any good, there is always the bad. Sometimes the angels become the demons. I have had my fair share of bad experiences on-line. These have occurred over the last few years. I had a cyber stalker. This person created a fake page and used my name and pictures. They wrote horrible things on it. They also tormented my mother. Nobody messes with my mama. Grr! It was absurd and ridiculous. Thankfully, we had a good friend who was able to help us deal with the situation and put an end to it.

I have also come across a few users who prey on kindness. You know the type of people who have an agenda and seek you out to use and then discard. They suck you into their twisted game of deception all under the guise of friendship. Scamming and scheming is all they know. These people are masters of deception, wolves in sheep's clothing. They appear sweet and unassuming but much like the holly at Christmas they are poison They leave behind only carnage in their wake. They take hot crazy mess to a whole new and terrifying level.

My Granny always taught me to make sunshine out of rain. In some ways even the negatives are positives because through these experiences I have become more enlightened. I'm not the same gullible, sheltered waif I once was. My eyes are wide open. The girl that longed to see the best in people is still alive in me. I hope I never lose touch with her, her childlike exuberant sustains me. She's just older, wiser and more in tune with the ways of the world.

I'll end my saga by saying the internet is a paradox full of wonder and lackluster. It can be the great equalizer and the great enabler. I love it tremendously and abhor it whole heartedly. It will never take the place of reading a good book, a walk in the sunshine, a glass of sweet tea, traveling the globe, a warm hug, or spending time with those we love. But, it can be a place to connect, communicate, learn, create advocate and be entertained.

Oh and watch adorable cat videos. Meow!

# CHAPTER 9

# A THANKFUL HEART

Now to sound like Oprah here, but there is a lot to be said for gratitude. I think it's a virtue to be embraced. It's important to find joy in the mundane and worth in the little things. I'm convinced emotional well-being begins with gratitude. Here are a few things I am grateful for?

What's on your list?

1.  Nutella
2.  Nature (I am addicted to trees, sunshine and fresh air)
3.  My family and friends (they are all nuts, but keep me going)
4.  Books (I couldn't function without the escapism they provide)
5.  Music (hope is found between the notes)
6.  Hot baths (just add the bubbles)

7. Orange scented anything (okay, maybe, not anything)
8. My rock star cat (coming soon to a location near you)
9. Good health (knock on wood)
10. Words ( expression is life)
11. Love (what the world needs more of)
12. Art (take time for beauty)
13. Laughter (the ones that come from the belly are the best)
14. Colors (imagine if everything was just black and white)
15. Road trips (crank up the music and ride, baby, ride)

The list is endless.

# CHAPTER 10

## LIFE

I've learned that expectations can often lead to heartache. Assumptions can lead to misunderstandings. I try to adhere to the following rules, although I'm not sure "rules" is the right word. Live what you speak. Hope without reason. Love without conditions. Give without expectations. Dream without limitation, but never delude yourself. Be, and let be. Of course, maybe, I am full of sh\*\*. Kicking boxing, hiking, and darting throwing can't hurt either.

I've also learned:

1. Be comfortable in your skin. Live fearlessly. Know what you want. Embrace your passions.
2. Be an original. Remember there is nobody else like you. Don't let others define your

worth. Define yourself! Write your script. Make it a masterpiece.

3. Every human life has value. We're all equal. When the rights of one are violated, so are the rights of all. Be a voice for love and humanity. Do more. Expect more. Be more.

4. Worrying and obsessing over a problem is a waste. Use that time to work on fixing the issues and brainstorming solutions. In between, perhaps, eat a scoop of Rocky Road or have a good workout session with a punching bag. (Note: The punching bag should not be someone's face!)

5. Having hopes and dreams is wonderful. However, making those hopes and dreams a reality through hard work and determination is the stuff of which dreams are made.

6. Be kind.

7. A world without love is like a book without words, a box without chocolate, hope without faith. Empty.

8. "This too shall pass" See. This list is just about over.

9. Perhaps, we shouldn't be offended by song lyrics, or a piece of art. The world would be a far better place if we were more offended by poverty, war, greed, social injustices.

10. Every day is a new day and a chance to begin again to love the ones you adore, to count

your blessings, to dance around the kitchen barefoot with the music blaring, to make up silly songs about your rock star cat, to eat another piece of chocolate, to read an amazing piece of literature, and to realize life is beautifully complex, but simple too.

TOSHA MICHELLE

# CHAPTER 11

## BEAUTY AND THE SELF-CONSCIOUS BEAST

Imperfection and flaws are beautiful no matter how strange or dysfunctional they may be. We all strive for perfection, but it is an unattainable, elusive dream. OK, unless you are Timothy Olyphant! Hubba, friggin' hubba. But I digress....

We all have things we would like to change about ourselves. Learning to accept that we are perfectly imperfect is the key to peace of mind and giving our mirrors a much-needed reprieve. Let's own our flaws and make them fabulous. Idiosyncrasies should be embraced. How boring life would be without them.

We women especially put so much effort into our hair, makeup and dress, setting such a high standard by comparing ourselves to others when we should just learn to love ourselves for who we are, flaws and all. Those flaws are what make us uniquely us. Let's learn to be confident in our insecurities. Our fears do not define our worth, nor naysayers out to cast their stones. Let's declare our independence from self-doubt. Remember, under all those gorgeous dresses, lovely hats, and winning smiles, even Kate Middleton probably has a few quirky qualities about her, like drinking milk straight from the carton, or something deranged like that.

# CHAPTER 12

## THE PROMISE OF PIXIE DUST

Being sensitive and in tune with the world can be very painful. There's so much suffering. It's hard not to drown in sorrow, in both our own and others. However, the only way to be is to feel, to give, to love. The challenge is not in the feeling. No, the test is learning how to navigate the highs and lows of life's tide, to understand, not only our frailties, but the frailties of others; to embrace the pain, but never lose sight of hope and the healing powers of love.

Wearing our hearts on our sleeves is dangerous. We run the risk of having them knocked off and broken. But I'd rather take that chance than keep my heart closed off from the world. I just want to feel, live and BE (and eat chocolate, hang out with Jon Stewart and listen to Justin Bieber tunes while solving math problem). Okay, well, maybe not those last two.

# CHAPTER 13

## WHO'S AFRAID OF THE BIG BAD...... BIG BIRD???

I've been doing a lot of soul searching recently, stripping away layers to find out who I am at the core. Turns out, I like to get my freak on, baby! Wiggle, wiggle, wiggle...Yeah...Umm, OK. You got me. Getting my freak on consists of being a neat freak, reading and writing for hours on end and bed at 10:00. It must be noted, I have been known to eat raw cookie dough and forgo making the bed. Wild women do, and they don't regret it. I'm losing the plot here though.

When I laid my soul bare, I found that fear has been the great motivator most of my life. As a child I was always anxious, scared of the dark, monsters under my bed, people. I was painfully shy. I was afraid of getting lost or being abandoned. It didn't help that I was sick a lot and had childhood epilepsy. Long story, but I was born premature, and in addition to causing damage to my optic nerve, it also affected another part of my brain. I was lucky I grew out of the seizures but my eyes are still a hot mess. In addition to all that nonsense, I also had an irrational fear of Big Bird. Yes, THE Big Bird from Sesame Street. His yellow feathers sparked terror in my young heart. It should be noted I was weird. The more things change.

As a teen, the fears differed but were just as strong. I was afraid of rejection, failure, not fitting in; I was still painfully shy and awkward. My irrational fears as a teen, boys. Yes, boys. I love them, but they became the new Big Bird. I had no clue what to do with their feathers except maybe ruffle them. I'm still a pro at that, by the way. I remember the great Dr. Suglia describing me this way: "girlishly charming and appealing but a trichotillomania inducing pill". (Screw you Joseph) ☺

As an adult, I figured boys out (sort of) but the fear of rejection and failure are still alive in me. I've learned to fake being outgoing. I push myself daily to live outside my comfort zone. However, the hills are still alive with the sounds of that anxious, shy, scared little girl. Nowadays, I find myself wondering why I have such extreme highs and lows. Life is wonderful. Life is horrible. This narrative is on an endless repeat like a bad mix of an Adele song. (By the way, how dare anyone mix an Adele song! THE NERVE!) The wonderful thing about reflecting and looking at one's soul is it leads to awareness. I've finally discovered the root of my neurotics. My moods are tied to outside forces. If I received praise that day, or if I felt slighted, if the scales were kind to me that morning or if they screamed (lay off the chocolate, woman) etc. I finally get it! I've been tying my worth to things and other people. I've been so consumed with the exterior; with wanting to be liked, wanting to fit in that I forgot to take inventory of the internal.

Guess what? The fear is coming from me; turns out I have had the power to dissolve it all along. All I had to do is find its source, acknowledge it, and kick in the teeth. So what if my charm eludes some people? So what if the scales go up a few pounds? So what if I don't fit some preconceived mold? My happiness, your happiness comes from within. We define who we are. No one else! The external will always be chaotic and unstable. People will come and go. Those things are out of our control. What we can control is ourselves and our reactions to life's lunacy and A-holes. The amazing thing is once we find peace with our inner being, the less shaky the exterior becomes. We have to let go of that which we cannot control.

Another secret I'm learning is the past and future are way overrated. The here, the now, this moment is what should really rock our socks off. When we focus on the present and what it can bring, fear becomes less and joy becomes more. I'm learning to kick that tired, worn narrative of I love my life-I hate my life to the proverbial curb.

Today I'm writing a new story, one of hope, self-expression and love. Fear has no place here. Living does. Now, if you'll excuse me, I'm going to find a grown boy and see if Sesame Street is on. Big, yellow, and his beautiful feathers are calling my name. (And no, that is not a euphemism.)

# CHAPTER 14

## SAGE WISDOM (COUGH, COUGH)
## BY YOURS TRULY

1. On the days you can't seem to please anyone, please yourself.
2. Everyone has baggage. It's just that some of ours come in a carry-on while others come in a tank of a suitcase.
3. You can never change a man so don't even try. Love him as he is and save your energy for more important endeavors: like eating Godiva, shopping, and hiding his body.
4. Justice may be for all but seldom is.
5. Childbirth is a walk in the park compared to child rearing.
6. Less fear. More action.
7. Music can soothe the soul unless it is hip hop; then I just want to brain someone.
8. When in Hot Topic, be sure to distinguish between the door and glass window before

charging toward what you think is the exit. Trust me. Your head will thank you. Also, take along a friend and children who will actually stop you from the aforementioned instead of laughing at you like you are the funniest thing since Bridesmaids, the movie. OK, never mind, that film was terrible, but you get the point.

9. Unsolicited advice is rarely appreciated unless the person you are giving it to is hammered at the time.

10. Wearing freakishly high heels to a standing-room-only concert is never a good idea; just ask my feet.

11. Kindness is more important than having the last word, unless you are dealing with a jerk. In that case, go ahead get in the last dig!

12. Money does not buy happiness, but it can buy a boatload of chocolate.

13. Love, not time, heals all wounds.

14. Bitterness and resentment will destroy your soul. Let it go!

15. I can't help how I feel, but I can help how I act on my feelings.

16. Accept and value yourself. This will bring you happiness. Embrace the good and the bad. I think we will always care what others think of us. But the key is to stop worrying

about it and live our lives on our terms. Love the ones who matter. Leave out the rest.

17. It's not what you say, it is what you do. So carry a big stick. I know, Huh???

18. No matter how much you care, some people are just A-holes.

19. If you are a celebrity, sadly, you can get away with pretty much anything.

20. Southern girls do it better. Note: I am not sure what "it" is, but trust me, we do it better!

21. Sweet tea goes with anything.

22. Cats only want attention when you are sleeping, reading, writing a paper, or doing chores.

23. By the way, my cat is a rock star.

24. Reading is fundamental, but math will get you the high paying jobs.

25. There is beauty in imperfection.

26. Growth only comes through change; or eating tons of chocolate.

27. Every day you should reach out and touch someone, just be prepared to be slapped.

28. It is more important to be lovable than loved.

29. In order to get along with your obnoxious, elitist, know-it-all of a neighbor, pretend they're someone else's.

30. Robert Frost was right, "Life goes on."

TOSHA MICHELLE

# CHAPTER 15

## IT'S OK

If your New Year's resolution doesn't get any deeper than conditioner... If Pier One Imports is your happy place... If you secretly crave Godiva chocolate, horde Godiva chocolates and hide Godiva chocolates from your family's grubby little hands (They're mine I tell you. MINE)... If you read Fifty Shades of Grey and liked it... (I mean I didn't of course, but if you did it's OK...No shame. ;)) If you secretly long to be a warrior princess but are more of a nerdy chick who gets lost in her own head and parking lots... If you get a little freaked out by escalators... (Escalaphobia is real, people. Down with judgment ...up with awareness... down with misconceptions...up with facts...is anyone else dizzy?) ...It's also OK to love without conditions ...to dream without limitations ... to hope without expectations and to live without fear.

It's not OK to shorten words into monosyllables…I mean that is just cray, bae. 'Kay?

# CHAPTER 16

## TALES FROM THE DORK SIDE

Back in my day, wow, did I just start a sentence out that way. Please feel free to add a, "now sonny" to the beginning. Anyway, where was I? Oh, yeah, back in my day sonny, there once lived a shy, awkward, geeky, little girl. This girl who, OK, just so happened to be yours truly, was constantly teased and picked on. I didn't fit in. I had these lovely coke bottle glasses. I was skinny as a rail, clumsy, and quite frankly, a little strange. I know, the more things change......

There weren't many days when I didn't come home from school crying because someone had called me a name or shunned me. I was bullied. I know that now. There are many stories I could share with you about that time, but I'd rather not dwell on it. My two saving graces were, I was a good student and I had a nice voice. I found a home in chorus. However, even that was riddled with problems. My choir teacher who was wonderful, and a real task master, was always pushing me to do solos and come out of my shell. I wanted to. I found solace in music, but at the same time, I was just too timid and insecure to even try. It was safer being in the background. I didn't want to call attention to myself. To do so was to risk ridicule.

Things starting changing for me in my senior year of high school. I was finally starting to develop curves and lose some of my awkwardness. However, the real turning point for me was college. It was sink or swim. College forces you to move and be. You either have to come out of your shell or get it smashed to bits. I was starting to gain some much needed confidence. I don't want to say, the ugly duckling became a swan, that sounds vain, but I did grow into my body, acquired some stylish glasses and became a better version of myself. I forced myself to talk to people. I had a boyfriend for the first time, a lovely guy name Matt. We formed a band, we would sing at festivals and the like. For the first time I felt free to be me. Oh, I was still strange. I always will be. I have always felt like I have one foot in this world, and the other in another. Today, though I embrace my uniqueness; I don't shy away from it.

My childhood was painful. I still to this day struggle with wanting to be liked. It doesn't take much for that shy, awkward little girl to rear her head, but in retrospect, it taught me some valuable lessons. Lessons that I try to impart to my children. Lessons like: know your own strength; never let anyone take away your self-worth. I encourage my girls to think outside the box and push them to be involved, to try out for solos, to talk to new people, and to embrace the things that make them special, not hide them away. They know that it's OK to be different. It's OK to speak your mind. It's OK to be YOU. Beauty, self-worth, and resiliency -- they all come from within. People will try and steal your bliss but as long as you love and respect yourself, they can never take your joy away.

TOSHA MICHELLE

# CHAPTER 17

# LIFE IN A FOREIGN LAND

"My wound is geography. It is also my anchorage, my port of call."

*I wrote this after my family moved to Texas from South Carolina. We are now back in the Palmetto State but I hope my experience can help someone who may be missing home.*

Coming to terms with my homesickness is a work in progress. Life is a series of transitional phases; I know change is inevitable. I consider myself a restless spirit who likes to roam. I am well-traveled, but my "port of call" has always been Carolina.

Going back home now is bittersweet. I take part in the activities and festivities that I took for granted before: family dinners, fireworks in the local park, eating at my favorite restaurant, walks in uptown Charlotte, weekend trips to Charleston and the Smokey Mountains, enjoying local treats, hours of gut-busting laughter with my mom, making music with my dad, seeing friends, going to the Comedy Zone, or hanging out at South Park Mall, listening to Bob and Sherri. I even miss our annoying pest of a neighbor.

Texas has been isolating in some ways. I feel out of my element, out of sync...out of step. Life is bittersweet but I refuse to dwell on the bitter, not when there's so much sweet to be found. I have my wonderful family by my side and, of course, Tucker -- Rock Star Cat Extraordinaire. I have dear friends and family, who may be far away but are near in spirit. Thank goodness, for Facebook and Skype. I have my nonprofit work that gives my life worth, a fun podcast that I host with my best gal pal, Jane... Soon, I will have a Master's. I'm looking forward to traveling to San Francisco this year, New England, and of course, back home. I'm trying to look at the move as a grand adventure. There's much to see and do here. Everything really is bigger in Texas. The people are friendly and the food is out of this world. I also know that this isn't my permanent home; that more changes are ahead. I welcome them with an open mind.

# CHAPTER 18

## LETTING GO

It's funny how we meet certain people and just know they are fated to be in our lives forever, but the universe has different plans. Reflecting back, I now understand that not all friendships are meant to last, although every friendship has a purpose. Friends come into our lives for a reason. They offer us just what we need at that particular moment. They help us grow...that growth could take a week, six months, or years. But when we have arrived at our spiritual destination it is time to move on, time to let go...Letting go is never easy. It hurts! But the best thing we can do for ourselves is to keep looking forward and believe that everything is as it's meant to be.

Letting go means letting go of fear, letting go of guilt, and letting go of blame. Don't be afraid to move on. People will always fall away, and sometimes they fall back. However, we have to live in the now, to know that for the time being we've learned all we can from them. Don't grieve for what is lost but rejoice for what was. Friendships are sacred and they reflect who we are. Just as we change, so do they. Things don't happen to us. They happen for us.

If there's one lesson life has taught me, it's that the only constants in this world are the hands of time and change... Roll with it...

# CHAPTER 19

## THE MORE THINGS CHANGE

"You can't stop the future. You can't rewind the past. The only way to learn the secret…is to press play."

Change is an organic thing that that happens every minute, every day, and everywhere. We as people are not meant to stay static. We may grow up but we should never stop maturing and expanding our hearts and minds. We shouldn't be held captive by the past or how people perceive us. We create and radiate our own unique way of being.

In some ways we are always changing but yet staying the same. When I look back at the me from yesteryear, I still see the same quirky, awkward, random, sentimental girl. I also see a woman who has a wealth of experience, who has endured illness, heartache and loss, but also experienced wonderful life-altering adventures. My journey has taken me out of my comfort zone and into a world of growth and enlightenment. It doesn't hurt that I have been blessed with the love and unwavering support of family and friends. These people teach me so much every day.

I still process information the same way, but experience has altered the way I interpret that information. Every day reveals a new layer of character. The years are teaching me and molding me into a better version of myself. I embrace getting older and look forward to one day being a, "wise old soul." Emerson said, "As we grow old the beauty steals inward." What a beautiful sentiment.

A work in process is what I will always be. I'm still evolving. I hope that never changes, even as I change. However, I know what I stand for and who I am. Uncertainty has no place in my inner world. It's a gift where decisions become easier, temptations become less, and confidence grows stronger.

Limitless

"For what it's worth: it's never too late or, in my case, too early to be whoever you want to be. There's no time limit, stop whenever you want. You can change or stay the same; there are no rules to this thing. We can make the best or the worst of it. I hope you make the best of it. And I hope you see things that startle you. I hope you feel things you never felt before. I hope you meet people with a different point of view. I hope you live a life you're proud of. If you find that you're not, I hope you have the courage to start all over again."

— Eric Roth, The Curious Case of Benjamin Button screenplay

# CHAPTER 20

# NEGATIVE PEOPLE SUCK

Feed your soul with positivity. People are so quick to spread hate and negativity. You can make a meal on that junk. It's so easy to get sucked into a vacuum of petty and destructive thoughts. Tune out the dysfunctional noise. Turn up the love. Negativity will always exist. Life by default comes with problems. No one has an easy road. We all have our own battles. However, we can choose to dwell in pain or live in peace. Your joy belongs to you. Don't ever give anyone the power to take it away.

Surround yourself with people who build you up. Loving your friends means wanting the best for them, building them up, celebrating their highs and helping them through the lows. True friendship is not a competition. Jealousy plays no part. True friendships are rooted in loyalty, honesty, and trust. True friends give without conditions. I'm thankful for my true friends, for their love, support and encouragement. Oh, and chocolate...always the chocolate.

It should be said. Love one another always, but don't forget to love yourself in the process. Slow down. Breathe. Listen to your inner voice. Sometimes, we have to take care of ourselves, before we can care for others.

# CHAPTER 21

## REBEL YELL

The mark of a true rebel (to me) is a person who fights against apathy, who embraces their humanity, and looks beyond the surface. It's easy to be mean-spirited, selfish, materialistic, and shallow. It takes heart and tenacity to embrace traits like honesty, integrity, compassion, kindness, and loyalty.

It's not about taking the moral high ground. No one is better than anyone else. We don't all have to believe a certain way, or be a certain way. But it sure would be nice if everyone could embrace love, forget about hate, and learn to live in harmony. Hey, a girl can dream. By the way, my rebel wears a suit, smells like Dior, and is handy with a wrench, a pen, and frying pan.

Anyway, gather round, children. Let's all hold hands, and sing a rousing rendition of Kumbaya.

# ACKNOWLEDGMENTS

I would like to thank you, the reader for taking a chance on my brand of silliness. I hope you enjoy my randomness.

If you did like the book and are so inclined, please consider leaving a review on Amazon, Barnes and Noble, and Good Reads. If you didn't like the book, keep that sh** to yourself. Just kidding.

I'd also be remiss if I didn't mention my beautiful family. They keep me sane when they aren't driving me up the wall. Special thanks to my editor Ron Barnett. Your insight was invaluable. To my beta readers and dear friends Larry White and Elena Totten. Thank you for your time and encouragement.

To Niles, thank God you finally shaved. I appreciate your face so much more now. Seriously, thanks for being one of my biggest champion.

To Jane ("You ignorant slut") I adore you. Heather, I have box of doughnuts with your name on it. Thanks for your humor and being all Canadian.

Lastly, to the pool boy gang: Diane, Donna, Jennifer, Sandy, Gabe, Amy, Laurel, Keith, Ian, and Trish. I love you all. Thanks for getting me.

# ABOUT THE AUTHOR

Tosha Michelle is a reformed Southern belle who lives to write and thrives on creatively, earning degrees and majoring in snark.

In her spare time, you can find her painting, singing, people watching, or hanging out with her family and rock star cat.

If you would like to keep up with her shenanigans, you can find her on Twitter at TaraLeigh2020 and musing on her blog at www.LaLiterati.com.